NERD
CULTURE

NERDING OUT ABOUT

GAMING

NERD
APPROVED
45TH PARALLEL
45°

VIRGINIA LOH-HAGAN

45TH PARALLEL PRESS

Published in the United States of America by Cherry Lake Publishing Group
Ann Arbor, Michigan
www.cherrylakepublishing.com

Reading Adviser: Beth Walker Gambro, MS, Ed., Reading Consultant, Yorkville, IL
Book Designer: Joseph Hatch

45th Parallel Press is an imprint of Cherry Lake Publishing Group.

Library of Congress Cataloging-in-Publication Data

Names: Loh-Hagan, Virginia, author.
Title: Nerding out about gaming / Virginia Loh-Hagan.
Description: Ann Arbor, Michigan : 45th Parallel Press, 2024. | Series:
   Nerd culture | Audience: Grades 4-6 | Summary: "Nerding Out About Gaming
   covers the wonderfully nerdy world of gaming: from boardgames to
   videogames. This 45th Parallel hi-lo series includes considerate
   vocabulary and high-interest content"-- Provided by publisher.
Identifiers: LCCN 2023035096 | ISBN 9781668939345 (paperback) | ISBN
   9781668938300 (hardcover) | ISBN 9781668940686 (ebook) | ISBN
   9781668942031 (pdf)
Subjects: LCSH: Games--Juvenile literature.
Classification: LCC GV1203 .L59 2024 | DDC 790.1/922--dc23/eng/20230821
LC record available at *https://lccn.loc.gov/2023035096*

Cherry Lake Publishing Group would like to acknowledge the work of the Partnership for 21st Century Learning, a Network of Battelle for Kids. Please visit Batelle for Kids online for more information.

Note from publisher: Websites change regularly, and their future contents are outside of our control. Supervise children when conducting any recommended online searches for extended learning opportunities.

Printed in the United States of America

Dr. Virginia Loh-Hagan is an author and educator. She is currently the Director of the Asian Pacific Islander Desi American (APIDA) Center at San Diego State University and the Co-Executive Director of The Asian American Education Project. She lives in San Diego with her very tall husband and very naughty dogs.

TABLE OF CONTENTS

Nerds are now trendy. Being a gamer is cool!

LIVING THE NERDY LIFE

It's finally cool to be a nerd. Nerd culture is every-where. It's in movies. It's on TV. It's in video games. It's in books. Everyone is talking about it. Everyone is watching it. Everyone is doing it. There's no escaping nerd culture.

Nerds and sports fans are alike. They have a lot in common. Instead of sports, nerds like nerdy things. Magic is nerdy. Science fiction is nerdy. Superheroes are nerdy. Nerds obsess over these interests. They're huge fans. They have a great love for a topic. They learn all they can. They spend hours on their hobbies. Hobbies are activities. Nerds hang with others who feel the same.

Nerds form **fandoms**. Fandoms are nerd networks. They're communities of fans. Nerds host online group chats. They host meetings. They host **conventions**. Conventions are large gatherings. They have speakers. They have workshops. They're also called **expos**. Tickets sell fast. Everyone wants to go. Nerd conventions are the place to be.

Nerd culture is on the rise. It's very popular. But it didn't used to be. Nerds used to be bullied. They were made fun of. They weren't seen as cool. They'd rather study than party. This made them seem odd. They were seen as different. Not anymore! Today, nerds rule!

Gaming magazines have been around since the 1980s. They are filled with tips and reviews.

The first successful video game was *Pong*.

CHAPTER 1

GAME ON

People love playing games. Games are a form of playing. They have rules. They have unknown outcomes. They have elements of chance.

Some people love playing more than others. These people are gamers. They're part of game culture. Game culture is a community. Gamers spend hours playing. They play with others. They meet in person. They form online groups. They share a passion for games. They cheer each other on. They work together. They beat their enemies.

Gamers play different games. Some play **tabletop games**. Tabletop games are board games. They're played on tables. Gamers also play video games. Video games are played on devices.

Gaming is not cheap. Game consoles and games can be expensive.

There are many game **genres**. Genres are types. There are card games. There are dice games. There are war games. There are action games. There are adventure games. There are shooting games. There are fighting games. There are role-playing games.

Gaming is fun. It's also good for the brain. There are many benefits. Gamers make many decisions. They solve problems. They're creative. They're critical thinkers. They learn to respond quickly. They learn to work in teams. They build leadership skills. Playing games improves focus. It increases memory.

Some gamers become **developers**. Developers design games. They invent new ways to play. People love to play!

Dice were invented more than 5,000 years ago. These dice were made of bones.

CHAPTER 2

FROM PLAY TO PROFIT

All cultures have games. Games are a way to pass time. They provide time away from work. They're fun. They build community.

The first board games came from the **ancient** Near East. Ancient means from old times. The Near East is the area around ancient Egypt. These early games used dice. They were designed for 2 players.

Chess developed in ancient India. Playing cards and the game Go developed in ancient China. Checkers developed in ancient Egypt. These games are still played today.

Over time, countries invaded. They conquered other countries. They traded. Games spread around the world. More games were invented.

NERD LINGO!

BATTLE ROYALE: Battle Royales are a game type. Players battle each other. They battle to the death. There's only one winner. The winner beats everyone. The winner is the last player standing.

CAMP: Camp is a game tactic. Some players camp. This means they hide. They stay in one spot. They wait for enemies. Some players think camping is cheating.

CLANS: Clans are groups of players. They play online games together. They often compete together. Each member has special skills. They need each other to win. Clans are also called guilds.

EASTER EGGS: Easter eggs are hidden features. They're like inside jokes. They're like messages. They enhance game play. Players like to find them.

MOD: Mod stands for modification. Modification means change. Players make mods.

NOOB: Noob stands for "newbie." A noob is a new player. Noobs are learning the game. They play at low levels. Gamers call bad players noobs. This is a mean thing to say.

Games were played in homes. They were played at community events. Then game shops opened. **Arcades** opened. Arcades are places with many electronic games. Playing games became more public.

People added more rules. Gaming became a sport. Gamers played in **tournaments**. Tournaments are a series of contests. Players compete. They play to win. Today, gamers can earn lots of money. Playing games can be a career.

Video gaming is a big business. Millions watch gamers play. Some gamers are famous. They have many fans. But most gamers just love to play. They play for fun.

Some famous gamers, like Dan TDM, have YouTube channels.

Milton Bradley (1836–1911) was a U.S. businessman. He launched the board game industry.

CHAPTER 3

GAMEPLAY OPTIONS

There are different game types. Tabletop games are the original game culture. Before video, there were board games. Monopoly and Scrabble are examples. Families and friends played them. These family board games were easy to play. They could be enjoyed by all. They were very popular. They're also called party games.

War strategy games became trendy. Risk and Battleship are examples. People enjoyed games with themes.

There was a movement toward **Eurogames**. This started in the late 1970s. Eurogames are German-style board games. They're harder. They focus on getting resources. They have themes. They aren't based on luck. Players need strategy. Catan is the most popular example. More than 20 million people play Catan.

TOO NERDY!

Provo is in Utah. We Geek Together is a Provo game store. It's in a mall. It broke a world record. This happened in 2023. The store hosted the most people playing Dungeons & Dragons. At least 1,227 people played. Some players wore costumes. Players were of all ages. Andrew Ashby is the store owner. He said, "I've always wanted to host the biggest game of Dungeons & Dragons. But that was just kind of a silly dream." Ashby made his dream come true. He saved up money. He set up 200 tables. Each table had 7 players. It had a game master. It represented an area of the battlefield. All tables worked together. They fought in a giant epic battle. The goal was to beat Vecna. Vecna is an evil demon. Players filled the whole mall. Ashby said, "A world record here in Provo. It's the nerdiest world record ever!"

Role-playing games are also popular. These games have themes. Players play as characters. They act like their characters. Some players even dress like their characters. Role-playing games can be played in person. They can be played online.

Dungeons & Dragons (D&D) is the most popular example. Players create characters. They play in character. They go on **quests**. Quests are adventures. Players fight in battles. They fight monsters. They have powers. They earn points. **Game masters** (GMs) are in charge. They narrate the story. They decide the rules. They use dice to decide outcomes. A fan said, "It's not a game. It's a social experience."

There are popular movies and shows about Dungeons & Dragons.

Video games have exploded. Game **consoles** were invented in the 1970s. Examples are Nintendo, PlayStation, and Xbox. Consoles are devices. Players could play video games at home. They just needed consoles and a TV. This meant players could play for hours. They played whenever they wanted.

Anyone can play video games. They can play on their phones. Gamers play harder games. They require gear. Gear is costly. Video gamers need computers. They need devices. They need gaming chairs. They need controllers. They need headsets.

There are many types of video games. Players can complete challenges. They can battle. They can build. They can race.

Super Mario is the biggest video game series. There's even a Super Nintendo World at Universal Studios in California.

About 65 percent of gamers play with others either in person or online.

Early video games were designed for 2 players. These players had to be in the same room. Or players played against the computer.

The internet changed the game. Now players can go online. Many players can play at once. This is called **MMOG**. MMOG stands for massively multiplayer online game. These games are more fun. Players are connected. They play on the same network. They can play from anywhere. They can talk to each other. They work together. Or they compete against each other. They play in an open virtual world.

One of the best-selling games is *Minecraft*. *Fortnite* is another popular game. Millions of people play per month.

Video game tournaments became popular. Leagues formed in the 1990s. Gamers gathered to compete. This started in Germany and South Korea. This led to **esports**. Esports stands for electronic sports. They're organized MMOGs. Professional sports organizations formed esports teams. Colleges are forming teams.

Professional video gamers compete. They play in tournaments. They compete for big prizes. They can become famous. Esports is a big business.

Esports have millions of fans around the world. Fans watch **streaming** videos. Streaming lets people watch content on devices. Fans watch on Twitch or YouTube. They also go to live shows.

The League of Legends World Championship is like the Super Bowl of video games.

NERD TO KNOW!

Johnathan Wendel was born in 1981. He's from Missouri. He's the first gaming superstar. His game name is Fatal1ty. In high school, he played tennis. After practice, he played video games. He played for hours. He played on weekends. He got really good. He started competing in 1999. He played in the United States. He played in Asia. He played in Europe. He won many tournaments. He became a world champion. He set world records. He has the most World Championships. He won a lot of money. He helped make competitive gaming popular. He was in TV shows. He's in the International Video Game Hall of Fame. He's in the Esports Hall of Fame. He started his own companies. He makes gaming products. He manages esports teams. He loves gaming. He said, "I think anyone that gets to do what they love for a living has a dream job."

Many people think VR (virtual reality) gaming is the future of gaming.

CHAPTER 4

RELEASE YOUR INNER NERD

You, too, can be a gaming nerd! Try one of these activities!

HOST A GAME NIGHT!

Games are best when played with others. Game nights are fun. People gather. They play games. They hang out. Game nights are great for trying out new games. They're also great for playing favorite games.

Invite some friends over. Make sure you have the right number of players. Check the game. See how many players you need.

Assign someone to be the game master. The game master should learn the rules. This will save time.

Provide snacks. Provide drinks. Have people eat before or after playing. Avoid ruining your game pieces.

PLAY IN A TOURNAMENT!

Most gamers have a favorite game. They play this game a lot. They practice all the time. They become good players. If you're good, think about competing.

Look online. Search for local tournaments. Know the rules. Some tournaments require fees. Some have age requirements. Follow all the rules.

Plan ahead. If you win, you'll compete at higher levels. You may be there a while. Bring snacks. Bring water. Learn to manage stress. Take care of yourself.

Bring a friend. Have someone cheer for you.

Don't worry about winning or losing. Have fun. Learn from others. Keep trying. Keep competing.

Competitive gaming, or esports, is growing. Many high schools and colleges have esports teams.

INVENT YOUR OWN GAME!

Gamers have played many games. They know how games work. They figure out tricks. They add changes to games. They make games more interesting. If you're tired of just playing, invent a game. Take elements from your favorite games. Think about your favorite moves. Come up with a theme. Create rules. Create the materials. For video games, learn **coding**. Coding is creating instructions for a computer to follow.

The first game version is an **alpha**. Alpha is only known to you. It's your draft. It's incomplete. It's not ready to be played.

The next version is the **beta**. Beta is ready for testing. Players play. You take notes. You fix any mistakes. This helps you create the final product.

There are more than 2,000 video game design schools in the world.

NERDY TIPS!

TIP #1

AVOID BEING A TOTAL NOOB. BE PREPARED. DO YOUR HOMEWORK. READ THE GAME RULES. WATCH YOUTUBE VIDEOS. WATCH OTHERS PLAY.

TIP #2

PRACTICE TO BE A PRO. PICK ONE TYPE OF GAME. GET TO KNOW THAT GAMING GENRE. DEVELOP TACTICS. CONNECT WITH OTHERS. FOLLOW GAME PLAYERS ON TWITCH. TWITCH IS LIVE VIDEO STREAMING FOR GAMERS.

TIP #3

LEARN FROM GAME-PLAY. REFLECT AFTER EACH GAME. THINK ABOUT YOUR MOVES. THINK ABOUT WHAT YOU DID RIGHT. THINK ABOUT WHAT YOU DID WRONG. THINK ABOUT WHAT YOU COULD DO BETTER.

TIP #4

TAKE CARE OF YOUR BODY. USE A GOOD GAMING CHAIR. DRINK LOTS OF WATER. TAKE MANY BREAKS. SITTING TOO LONG CAN BE HARMFUL. REMEMBER TO GO OUTSIDE. GET SUNLIGHT. IT'S EASY TO LOSE TRACK OF TIME.

TIP #5

KEEP YOUR BRAIN SHARP. BRAINS ARE MUSCLES. KEEP THEM ACTIVE. DO PUZZLES. SOLVE RIDDLES. PLAY MUSICAL INSTRUMENTS. PLAY SPORTS.

GLOSSARY

alpha (AL-fuh) an early version of a program that is not to be released to the public, similar to a first draft

ancient (AYN-shuhnt) from a time long ago

arcades (ar-KAYDZ) places to play games on money-operated machines

beta (BAY-tuh) an early version of a program, after alpha, that is made available for testing by a limited number of users before its general release

coding (KOH-ding) creating computer instructions

consoles (KAHN-sohlz) electronic devices that output a video signal or image to display a video game that can be played with a game controller

conventions (kuhn-VEN-shuhnz) large meetings of fans who come together to talk about and to learn more about a shared interest

developers (dih-VEH-luh-perz) people who design or make things

esports (EE-sportz) electronic sports or organized online video games that can be played by a large number of professional gamers at the same time

Eurogames (ER-roh-gaymz) tabletop board games from Europe, specifically Germany, that revolutionized modern board game design

expos (EK-spohz) large public exhibitions

fandoms (FAN-duhmz) communities of fans; combines "fanatic" and "kingdom"

game master (GAYM MA-ster) a person who organizes and oversees a role-playing game by narrating the story and deciding the rules; shortened to GM (GEE EM)

genres (ZHAHN-ruhz) categories, types, or styles of artistic composition

MMOG (EM EM OH GEE) Stands for massively multiplayer online game, an online video game that can be played by a very large number of people at the same time

quests (KWESTS) adventures or journeys

role-playing (ROHL-play-ing) the act of pretending to be another character; shortened to RP (AR PEE)

streaming (STREE-ming) a method of transmitting or receiving data over a computer network

tabletop games (TAY-buhl-tahp GAYMZ) board games played on a table

tournaments (TER-nuh-muhnts) series of contests where players compete for big prizes

LEARN MORE

Duling, Kaitlyn. *Power On: The History of Gaming*. Vero Beach, FL: Rourke, 2021.

Esports: The Ultimate Guide. New York: Scholastic, 2019.

Hicks, Gabriel. *A Kid's Guide to Tabletop RPGs: Exploring Dice, Game Systems, Roleplaying, and More!* New York: Running Press Kids, 2021.

Ratcliffe, Amy. *A Kid's Guide to Fandom: Exploring Fan-Fic, Cosplay, Gaming, Podcasting, and More in the Geek World!* New York: Running Press Kids, 2021.

INDEX